From Darkness to Light

SPECKTRUM ART

SPECKTRUM ART

SPECKTRUM ART

SPECKTRUM ART

SPECKTRUM ART

<u>DEDICATION</u>

This book is dedicated to all who have or currently are going through a dark time in life. Writing and creating art has always helped me. I hope this collection will be able to help you in some way. Even if it's just a little.

SPECKTRUM ART

<u>ACKNOWLEDGMENTS</u>

A very special thank you to my mother, father, sister, grandparents and all other family members that have always been loving, understanding and supportive during this difficult but wonderful adventure called life.

Thank you to the friends I have made and lost along the way. You all made a difference and I am forever grateful.

Thank you to the kindhearted strangers I have encountered. I appreciate the small acts of kindness; they made the biggest difference in my times of need.

Thank you to all who have hurt me, been cruel and hateful towards me. You have shown me what I don't want to be and, in some way, helped shape me into the strong, kind and wise person I am to this day. So, thank you.

Last but most importantly, thank you to my other half – the absolute love of my life. I am so happy to have you as my partner in this life. You have been there at the darkest of times and helped me through my journey to the light. I have fallen in love with you, but you… you made me fall in love with myself and with life. Thank you, my love!

SPECKTRUM ART

<u>SECTIONS</u>

This book is divided into three different sections to help portrait my journey from darkness to light:

Black, Grey and White.

SPECKTRUM ART

SPECKTRUM ART

...

FROM DARKNESS TO LIGHT

...

SPECKTRUM ART

SPECKTRUM ART

SPECKTRUM ART

BLACK

SPECKTRUM ART

With time you can heal a broken heart,
but you can never fix a broken soul.

I'm sitting on my bed again,
staring at the walls and ceiling.
I just wish my mind could stop thinking,
that my internal wounds would start healing.
It's late at night
and the room is filled with silence.
The only sound is my heart beating
and my slow breathing.
The suffering inside of me
is tearing me apart.
These feelings just won't go away.
The pressure is building up in my heart.
I just want the pain to go away.
I just want the pain to go away…

To be your own worst enemy
is the biggest burden one can carry.

<u>Insecurities</u>

Do you ever ask yourself
if we are okay?
We're laying next to each other
but you feel so far away.

Your lips tell me
that you love me.
But your eyes
don't look at me the same.

Is it us,
are we just tired?
Or is it our love
that is slowly dying.

Behind this mask I am lost,
but I don't mind.
Without an identity,
I remain unreachable.
Without a surface,
I remain unbreakable.
Hidden behind this barrier,
my own creation.

I surrender

I surrender to the darkness
I'm finally letting go
I can't take it any longer
I can't live with a broken soul

I surrender to the feelings
That just won't go away
To the depression
That seems to want to stay

I surrender to the disease
That flows through my veins
To the words inside my head
That makes me go insane

I surrender to the physical pain
That occasionally allows me to be free
To all the tears that I shed
The sharp blades that make me bleed

...

...

I surrender to the suffering
For whom left me with a broken soul
To the ongoing pain
That makes me feel so alone

I surrender what's left of my broken soul
To the darkness that surrounds me
Suffocating me while holding me tightly
Not willing to let go

I surrender to the darkness
I'm finally letting go
I can not be saved
For I am a broken soul

I surrender

These feelings are not sudden,
they've been with me quite a while.
I don't let them see that I'm suffering,
I just hide it with a smile.

The Bully

Your insults are like bullets
and you are the ice-cold gun.
Your finger squeezing that trigger
shooting down victims for fun.
Preying on the weak, exploiting their defeat.
How does that make you feel better
or make you better than anyone?
Words hurt like knives.
They're not just words
when they're taking so many lives.
You're just there swinging that blade
hurting people one at a time.
You're in our schools and in our streets.
You are the bully.

The Witness

It wasn't your lips the insults came out of
but you just stood there and laughed.
It wasn't your fists that hit them
but you were standing at arm's length.
It wasn't you that killed them
but your silence was just a deadly.
They say words hurt like knives.
Maybe you weren't the blade
that cut the victim.
But last time I checked
the handle is still part of the weapon.
You may have kept your mouth shut
or looked the other way.
You may not be the bully,
but you are guilty just the same.

My mind is a little clouded.
My heart is a little torn.
My body is a little scarred.
My soul is a little worn.

<u>Illusion</u>

Take a good look at me,
tell me what do you see?
Do you see the illusion of myself
or can you see the real me?

When you listen to the sound of my voice,
do you notice my pain?
Can you listen past the illusion
or do you fall for it?

When you look into my eyes,
do you see my suffering?
Can you see what I'm going through
or is all you can see the illusion I create?

Do you think you really know me
or actually know what I feel?
Because I think that all you can see
is simply the illusion of me.

Take a good look at me,
tell me what do you see?
Do you see the illusion of myself
or can you see the real me?

<u>Alcohol</u>

I remember those nights
When I would turn to alcohol
Shot after shot
Drink after drink
I told myself
That I should keep going
Until I can no longer think
Until I can no longer feel
Yeah, I should keep going
Until there's more alcohol than blood
Inside my veins
Just one more shot
Just one more drink
Maybe it will be enough
To drown my thoughts
To drown my pain
Maybe the alcohol will be enough
To make it go away

We all have a mask.
Some wear a mask to hide who they are
or to be someone they are not.
Some wear a mask to hide how they feel
or to pretend to be feeling something.
We all have a mask.
One day that mask will break
and so will you.

Black.
There's nothing but black.
What I see.
What I feel.
The darkness grasped everything.
There's nothing left but black.

<u>All the scars</u>

All the scars I wear
I could tell you the story
Of every single one
Some from feeling nothing
Others for feeling too much
To punish myself
Or those that I love
To serve as a reminder
That the world isn't getting kinder
That I could do better
And I am not enough
All the battles I have fought
Some I lost
Some I won
All the scars that I wear
Are nothing compared
To those you can't see
Try not to judge
So easily

My will to fight is paper thin.
I'm hanging on to a string,
nothing but a string.
My insides are slowly fading.
I feel nothing,
I am nothing at all.

<u>Fading Away</u>

There is no god
There is no hope
She has no heart
She has no soul

She's just a hollow being walking around
Slowly fading away without a sound

Lightning strikes to the core
Incinerated by all the pain
Drowning due to tears
Buried beneath all the weight

She's always been broken from the start
Slowly fading away into the dark

System overload
Automatic shutdown
Forever lost
Never will be found

…

…

She's just a hollow being walking around
Slowly fading away without a sound

Her reflection in the mirror has disintegrated
As the pieces fall and shatter on the floor
The pieces fall around me as I collapse
I'm slowly fading away rest assured

She's always been broken from the start
Slowly fading away into the dark

I'm slowly fading away

Dark clouds that arise.
Darkness shall thrive
and take everything away.
I'm drowning in an ocean of despair,
reassurance isn't there.
Hopelessly sinking deeper
in this rough sea of gray.

Addiction That I Need

I like to see myself bleed,
it reminds me I'm still alive.
If ever I make it through,
how will I know I have survived?

I like to hear the tear,
as the blade separates my skin.
A battle between metal and flesh,
but the blade always wins.

I like to feel the pain,
to me it's a simple release.
As soothing as pouring rain,
it's an addiction that I need.

Anxiety is like a snake
Wrapped around your neck
The more you fight to breathe
The tighter that it gets

You know when you put a mask on
to hide who you really are?
Well I've left mine on for so long
that I just don't know how to take it off…

When I would pressure the sharp blade
To cut through my skin
I felt mostly physical pain
Yet it's impossible to numb the depression

She's always been broken.
Makes her more vulnerable to the darkness.
It never really leaves her,
occasionally just takes an absence.
Allowing her to breathe for a while.
Fear lingers within her,
the fear of the darkness
It always returns to strike her like lightning,
like a knife to the heart.
Surrounding her completely
and leaving her defenseless.
Unable to evade the black.

Do You Know What It's Like?

Do you know what it's like
when you're scared to see yourself?
When you're not who you want to be.
Do you know what it's like
when you wish you were someone else?
You are your own worst enemy.

The break of day
is only the beginning.
I fight until the break of dawn
and still don't know if I'm winning.

<u>Anxiety</u>

She will keep you locked
Inside of your head
She will pin you down
Onto your bed

She will tell you lies
And tell you some more
She will convince you
Not to walk out that door

She will make the simplest tasks
Seem so out of reach
She will show you that
The goals you set will not be achieved

She is the pain in your chest
She is the cloud in your head
She is unjustifiably
She is anxiety

We carry on our backs
The burdens that time always reveals

I keep everything bottled up inside
Until the end of the day
When it's dark and silent
During the night
I try to fight the tears
But they fall around me
Like pouring rain
All I want
Is for the suffering to go away
I just wish
I could stop the pain

Addiction

I may have your heart,
but she's always on your mind.
When things get hard you turn to her
and I get left behind.

She makes your heart beat faster
than I ever have.
She can take you higher
than I ever can.

She's persistent and determined
to keep you to herself.
As much as I love you, I can't save you.
Only you can save yourself.

She is in control.
She is toxic.
She is an infection.
She is addiction.

If all the words I write
could take the pain away,
I swear I'd write them all.
If every tear I shed
could make me feel lighter,
I swear I'd cry a waterfall.

Dark Thoughts

Blade between your fingertips
Rope around your neck
Bottle of pills inside your hands
Feet standing on the edge

Laying on the train tracks
Exhaust fumes filling up your lungs
Gun pressed to your head
Electronic on the side of the tub

You picture each and every one
Over and over again
Oh, the dark thoughts
Stuck inside your head

GREY

SPECKTRUM ART

Keep Fighting

Put down the blade
Remove the rope around your neck
Throw away the bottle of pills
Back away from the edge

Walk away from the train tracks
Breathe oxygen into your lungs
Lower the gun from your head
Get out of the tub

The pain won't last forever
Things truly do get better
I know because I made it
And you can make it too

For them, for us, for me, for you

Keep fighting.

Not Broken

When we hurt
We try to fix ourselves
But…
You can't fix something
That isn't broken
We just need time
To heal the wounds that are open
You're not broken

Never expect your love to be understood.
Never expect anyone to return it.
Just keep giving.

Hate lasts longer, but love is stronger.

Change of Melody

The beat of your heart has a darkened tune,
as silence becomes your worst enemy.
Your thoughts take over, as does the agony.
The colors around you slowly fade to grey,
everything slowly fades to grey…
Eyes are the window to the soul,
but what can we see if your window is closed?
Push away your fears,
open your window and shout if you have to!
Just let it all out.
You are not alone.
Time will teach you to let go of the pain,
of the regrets.
To embrace the silence
and to listen for your heart's color filled beats.
With that different melody around you,
you will realize that at that moment…
You are free.

There's this grey area
that people don't talk much about.
When you've started healing
but are having doubts.
Am I getting better?
Will I find the way out?
Do I keep going?
Should I give up now?

45

I wish I was a hero
Not the kind that wears a cape
But the kind that could help you
Take the pain away

The System is Broken

Mental health is important
But the system is broken
You reach out your hand
But they tell you to wait
Before they're ready to hold it
They put your name on a list
But the list is so long
That you don't know
If you'll be able to hold on
When your turn comes
They tell you to take a seat
They tell you to speak quickly
Because they have more people to see
Then the world wonders why
There are so many of us
Trying to end our own lives
You wake up in a hospital
Doctor walks in and sighs
He makes it clear that your case
Is just a waste of time
Doesn't ask any questions
Just tells you
If you want to end your life
There's nothing he can do

…

...

So you keep your mouth shut
When you're released from the hospital
You're back to square one
So, we stop reaching out
And don't put our names on lists
We stop seeing so called professionals
Because we know how it is
Mental health is important
But the system is broken

I can't seem to understand
why I feel the way I do.
I don't think I'll ever understand,
I just hope I can make it through.

The blood in my veins is tainted,
at least that's what they say.
I am told I should get some help,
I should get on my knees and pray.
Religion is a choice created by man,
something taught along the way.
People like me of the rainbow community,
we were all born this way.
So, tell me again what is unnatural?

A cloudy mind and heartache
Forecast is saying it will be a long day

A cry for help is often quiet
Most people will try to hide it
A soft whisper when you're asleep
Or a letter you'll never read

Hero & Sidekick

I am not a hero
But I promise I'll be right beside you
While you're fighting to save yourself

You will need to wear the cape
But I promise you will never be alone
While you're conquering your hell

Some battles will be difficult
But I promise I'll steady your hand
As you are facing your demons

The days you feel like you won't make it
I promise to surround you with my love
And remind you of all the right reasons

One day you will hang your cape
We will smile hand in hand
I will look at you and say

You won, you made it
You are the hero
And I am your sidekick

53

Animals may not be able to communicate, but they still understand when you're not doing ok.

<u>Fighter</u>

I'm no longer ashamed of my scars
but it's not something to make light of.
No, I didn't get scratched by a cat
and didn't get mauled by a tiger.
You may think I'm weak
but I assure you I'm a fighter.

55

To be kind beyond words
To give of yourself until it hurts

<u>Family</u>

Dear mother,
Dear father,
Dear sister,

I am sorry I caused you pain
When I was in a dark place
I was just trying to get rid of my own

You showed me love
You showed me patience
You showed me understanding

I know that you recognized
That I wasn't a difficult child
I was just going through a hard time

You taught me strength
You taught me courage
You taught me wisdom

I will never forget
All that you have done for me
I am so proud to have you as my family

Don't wait
If there's something you want
Do it today

When I was hospitalized
It made me realize
I didn't really want to die
I just needed help

Dear Stranger,

I hope you are out of danger
I hope you find the strength
To face your fears
And fight off your demons
I hope the cloud over your head disappears
And that you can hold on
To a reason
To stay

I promise everything will be okay.

I've worked so hard to be better
and you deserve the absolute best of me.
Right now I'm a little under the weather
and right now you're the best of me.

Sometimes you need to lose yourself
In order to find yourself.

We

We are all unique
We all feel
We all think
We all heal
We all break
Differently
We are not all the same
There is no scale to measure
Depression
Anxiety
Suicidal thoughts
Agony
We all suffer some form of pain
Hers not worst than his
Yours not worst than mine
We all have a hell to go through
And demons to fight
We all love
We all hate
We all fight
We all fail
Differently
But we are all in this just the same

Despite that life is complicated,
that my world is dark and grey.
I hope for light to find me,
to help me find my way.

I am not the best daughter.
I am not the best sister.
I am not the best lover.
I am not the best friend.

All of you make up the best
parts of what I am.

Reason to Stay

If you can't live for yourself
live for someone else.
For your parents, siblings, lover, friends, pets…
If you can't live for yourself
live for them.

Demons

The demons that haunt you
I know that they want you
But I want you more

My love will be your armor
I will be your shield
And your sword

When the devil
Comes for you himself
I will be the walls to your castle

Every cell of my being
Soldiers for you my queen
That will help you fight your battles

One day you'll make it out of your hell
Even with all your demons ringing the bell
You'll be looking at me

As long as we're in it together
We can face anything
For true love conquers all you see

I hate being alone
Because loneliness is all I feel
I enjoy all moments of silence
It allows my wounds to heal

Keep Quiet

Children should be taught about emotions
And how to deal with what they're feeling
Mental health shouldn't be a subject so taboo
It should be talked about at home and school
From such a young age
Kids are told to be good
And be sure to make good grades
When they try to express how they feel
Parents say they're busy or had a long day
Children are told to keep quiet
And to go play in their rooms
So, that's what they do
The years go by and the children grow older
They still don't know what to do
With the feelings in their hearts
And the weight on their shoulders
Teens do their best to fit in
With the people they call friends
When they try to open up
They are told they are downers
They are encouraged to stay home
And to keep quiet
So, that's what they do

…

...

Days turn to weeks and
Weeks turn to months
All those teens into young adult
Isolation and tears
The pain from all those years
One day they'll decide it's enough
It's no surprise so many people
Choose to end their own lives
And then
Family, lovers, friends
All wonder why
They didn't reach out
They didn't ask for help
They chose to keep quiet
Yeah, they chose to keep quiet

Black, Grey, White.
This is the journey from darkness to light.

I am thankful for those
Who were kind to me
I am thankful for those
Who were not

The Road to Recovery

The road to recovery
Is different for everybody
Some need to heal externally
Others internally
We need to find what helps us
As individuals
There is no magical cure
That is universal
There is no simple path
That we can all take
We need to learn
To find our own way
Some may need to do it alone
Others may need some help
Trained professionals, medication,
Therapy, meditation,
New experiences, new faces
In order to heal your wounds
Follow the road to recovery
That is best for you

SPECKTRUM ART

WHITE

You are the bow
The arrow is your life
Which direction it goes
Only you can decide

Beautiful Paradise

The stars seem so bright, so perfectly aligned
They softly whisper into the night
Can't resist to break the silence
With sweet words, we begin to drift closer

The wind carefully dies down
As we feel summer's heat all around us
Leaves dance and twirl, so do we
To the rhythm of our hearts beating as one

Ocean waves upon the shore, leaving a mark
That my fingertips trace all over your body
Every curve, every sway
They faithfully follow in a loving caress

As we close our eyes, we collide
Like two puzzle pieces, perfection at it's best
Every second together can only bring us closer
Holding you in my arms, our souls intertwined

Having your lips on mine
Such a beautiful paradise

When you sail out to sea
I long for the day you come back to me
Like the waves
They always go back to the shore
I will love you forevermore

Be wise
Be kind
Have an open heart
And an open mind

Let Me

Let me be the pillar you can lean on
When you're falling apart
Let me be the shoulders that help you
Carry the weight
Let me be the arms that shield you
From a world filled with hate
Let me be the hands you reach for
When you're feeling insecure
Let me be the footprints you follow
When you are unsure
Let me be the ears that listen
When you have something to say
Let me be the lips that tell you
Everything will be okay
Let me be the light
That guides you out of the dark
Let me help you be free
Let me be everything
That you may need

Never let other people's words define you.
Only you can define yourself.

<u>Little Things</u>

When life gets too hard
Concentrate on the little things
How the flowers bloom at sunrise
How peacefully the birds sing

When you feel like you're falling apart
Concentrate on the little things
How the stars light up the night
How good it feels with the sun on your skin

When your heart is slowly breaking
Concentrate on the little things
The feeling of a nice warm bath
The comfort a cup of tea can bring

When you're running out of reasons to stay
Concentrate on the little things
Accumulate as much as you can
You will see the beauty life can bring

You're the arrow to my compass
And the beat of my heart
You're the chills on the surface
And my sky filled with stars

If the least I can do
Is put a smile on someone's face
Then I've accomplished something wonderful
The smallest of things
Can make a big impact in someone's life

Lay Here

As the morning light settles in,
It caresses your skin
I awaken to your beautiful smile
Oh, the dimples in your cheeks drive me crazy
Let's just lay here for a while

My arms gently wrapped around you
Your fingertips tracing my curves
Going down my spine
These simple little things
That can make you lose your mind

You're lying right next to me
Yet I'm aching to have you closer
As our bodies gently collide
Your lips fit perfectly on mine
I can't imagine it get's better

Feeling my skin against yours
Wrapped in a sea of blankets
Our hips gracefully sway
To the rhythm of our hearts
You completely take my breath away

Keep me your prisoner
This is the sweetest surrender I've known
Your beautiful smile has me confined
Oh, the dimples in your cheeks drive me crazy
The definition of love has been redefined

Let's just lay here for a while

It's just two lines on paper,
But it's meaning is far greater.
Equal.
Equality.

Everything

When you truly love someone,
that they are in possession of your heart.
No wonder it's so painful to be apart.
Your heart is a vital part of your being.
You've become much more than that,
you're my everything.

Pull me close
And I'll pull you even closer
The look in your eyes
I swear is the sweetest torture

Scars

I used to be ashamed
Of all my scars
But not anymore
Now I trace my fingertips
Over them and smile
They are a reminder
Of all I have gone through
And that I survived
We all have scars
Some on the surface
Some on the inside
Don't be ashamed
Be proud of your scars
They helped shape you
Into who you are

The sound of silence
That empty feeling
Only you can fill

I have known enough hatred
To know how to spare it
I have known enough kindness
To know how to share it

<u>Legend of The Phoenix</u>

Such a beautiful bird
A creature out of this world
Flames for feathers
And a fiery soul

So many years of being strong
Soaring high above us
It sings a sad song
Where no one can hear

As powerful as it may seem
The phoenix can only take so much
After so many years
It will burn itself up

Here it is
From the ashes it has risen
A rebirth, a second chance
Something that will free it

This is the legend of the phoenix

The light of day has faded away
By now the darkness of night has taken over
The stars light up the sky
Now it seems the sky is falling
As we close our eyes
We collide

Invincible

Raise your fist,
Raise your pride.
Show the world your true colors inside.
Show the world how much you stand out.
Don't be afraid to be yourself.

Raise your flag,
Raise your awareness.
Let the world know you've had enough.
Let the world know you don't want to suffer.
Don't be afraid you're not alone.

Raise your head,
Raise it high.
Show the world that you're not giving in.
Show the world how strong you really are.
Don't be afraid you're invincible.

Even with a million scars
She sees them as a million stars
You trace the constellations
All the way to my heart

Would you be mine?

Since the first day I saw you, our eyes first met
My heart knew something that I didn't know yet
Like the way the waves are drawn to the shore
Never have I felt this way before

Oh, when she hold's me down
I can feel my body lifting off the ground
Darling, keep me your prisoner
This is the sweetest surrender I have found

I want to explore every inch of your body
Every inch of your mind
You attract me in ways
That even I can't define

There are those who follow their dreams
And those who follow their hearts
I'd give them all away
To be where you are

You make me lose my senses
And the notion of time
From now until forever
Darling, will you be mine?

Your gentle breaths brush my neck
and sends chills down my spine.
Our lips fit perfectly together
as our bodies collide.

Girl in The Mirror

I used to tell her I hate her
I used to tell her she's worthless
I used to hurt her as much as I could
And tell her she deserved it

Now I tell her I love her
Now I tell her she has worth
Now I am kind to her
And tell her it's what she deserves

I used to tell her she's ugly
I used to tell her she's a disease
I used to tell her she has no place in this world
And that she should leave

Now I tell her she's beautiful
Now I tell her she's unique
Now I tell her she belongs in this world
And tell her this is where she should be

I'm standing here looking at her
Oh, how we have changed
The girl in the mirror
She and I have come a long way

Dear lover,
One of the greatest gifts
You have given me
Was how to love myself

<u>Poetry</u>

A warm cup of tea
Pencil in my hand
And a notebook on my knee

Collection of words
That perfectly describe
How I feel

Beautiful artform
An outlet, a savior
To help me

This is poetry

As I was searching for myself
I stumbled onto you

<u>One Year</u>

Already a year has passed since the day
You said you'd be mine, we became one
Our hearts synced and grew stronger
Oh darling, so did our love

From the very first time our eyes met
To the first touch and our first kiss
The first "I love you", every second with you
Has been nothing but perfect and bliss

Although we have fought
Had our ups and downs
We easily could have walked away
But chose to stay and stand our ground

To travel the world
Or to lay underneath a blanket of stars
My favourite place will always be
Wherever you are

Now I know this is forever
And I wouldn't want it any other way
I love you more than ever
Happy one year anniversary

Positivity is key
To true happiness
To true love
To finding your true self

My favorite place on earth
Will always be HER.

Tell Me

Tell me all the things I want to hear
That all my sorrows will disappear
Tell me the sun will rise and the moon will fall
That after darkness comes light after all
Tell me everything will be alright
That you will always be by my side
Tell me that all the clouds will part
That the rain will have to stop
Tell me you want to kiss me
That your arms will always reassure me
Tell me the birds shall sing
That they do so every morning
Tell me I am beautiful
That I should believe you because you're
truthful
Tell me even after the harshest of winters
That the flowers bloom more beautiful than
ever
Tell me you love me, please tell me again
Tell me that you'll never let me forget

As I gently lay my head
Where your shoulder meets your neck
You press your lips on mine
As I trace your heart upon your chest

It's crazy how your heart
Contradicts your mind
Of the things you know
You can't deny

Ten Years

Ten years
Ten years and I'm still here
It was in March 2009
I wanted to end the pain
I tried taking my own life
I'm happy that I stayed
I chose to fight
And got the help that I needed
I have gone through hell
And fought against my demons
Honestly, some days I still do
But with time it gets easier
For those who are hurting
Believe me when I say
Things will get better
As I am living proof
Ten years
Ten years and I'm still here
So are you
Keep fighting
I promise you'll make it through

I want to see the world through your eyes
In exchange I'll let you see through mine

The clock on the wall
How I wish it would stall
When you're peacefully asleep
In my arms

<u>What is Love?</u>

How am I to define it
There aren't enough words to describe it
A feeling deep inside
That can also be seen on the surface

You can see it in your eyes
In your smile
You can feel it in your heart
In your mind

It can be a feeling,
A person or a place
It has many different forms
And many different shapes

Love is pure
Love is beautiful
Love is for all
Love is eternal

Once you get out of the darkness
And into the light
You will see the true meaning
The beauty of life

SPECKTRUM ART

<u>ABOUT THE AUTHOR/ARTIST</u>

I grew up in the wonderful small town of Cap-Pele, NB, Canada. I am currently living in another beautiful small town of Bathurst, NB, Canada. I enjoy a little bit of everything in life. I love art in all of its forms (poetry, drawing, painting…). I enjoy gaming out, watching movies and reading. I also enjoy hiking, camping and kayaking. I love cooking and food even more. I am a big fan of tattoos. I enjoy spending time with family and friends when I can. I love my fur babies. Most of all I love my wife, my other half, with all my heart!

-K.

Dear Reader,

Thank you for taking the time to read this book!

I am no Picasso or Shakespeare, but I have enjoyed creating art for as long as I can remember and am proud of what I create. My intention is to share this collection with the world so that it can hopefully help someone, somewhere out there.

Sincerely,

-K.

Follow my journey through art and poetry!

 specktrum.art@gmail.com

 SpecKtrum Art

 specktrum.art

 SpecktrumA

www.ingramcontent.com/pod-product-compliance
Lightning Source LLC
Chambersburg PA
CBHW031340060726
47590CB00007B/2560